RECLAIM YOUR JOY

365 AFFIRMATIONS FOR LIBERATION AND TRANSFORMATION

ALESHA R BROWN

Reclaim Your Joy: 365 Affirmations for Liberation and Transformation

©2024 Alesha R. Brown

Published in Hampton, VA, by Fruition Publishing Concierge Services®. Fruition Publishing Concierge Services® is a division of Alesha Brown, LLC.

Fruition Publishing Concierge Services® can bring authors to your live event. For more information or to book an event, visit Fruition Publishing Concierge Services® at:

www.FruitionPublishing.com

ISBN: 978-1-954486-56-0 eBook

ISBN: 978-1-954486-57-7 Paperback

Library of Congress Control Number: 2024926452

FRUITION
PUBLISHING
CONCIERGE SERVICES®

FRUITIONPUBLISHING.COM

A DIVISION OF ALESHA BROWN, LLC

CONTENTS

INTRODUCTION

Welcome, Joy-Seekers!

If you're holding this book in your hands (or device), let me say this: you are already on the path to transformation. This is your time to reclaim your joy, power, and the beauty of your life, step by step, one day at a time.

Let's face it—life has a way of piling up on us. Between the demands of our daily routines, the weight of unspoken expectations, and the emotional residue of past wounds, it's easy to feel disconnected from our purpose, dreams, and even ourselves. That's why I created this book.

Reclaim Your Joy: 365 Affirmations for Liberation and Transformation is not just a book; it's a companion, a cheerleader, and a daily dose of inspiration to guide you back to yourself. Through these affirmations and simple, actionable steps, you'll reconnect with your inner strength, rediscover the beauty in your life, and create lasting change.

Joy is not something you wait for—it's something you create. It's in the way you speak to yourself, the choices you make, and the love you pour into your life every single day. This book will remind you that joy is always within reach, even in the smallest, quietest moments.

HOW TO USE THIS BOOK

This book is designed to fit into your life—not the other way around. Whether you're carving out five minutes in the morning with a cup of coffee or ending your day with quiet reflection, you can engage with these affirmations in a way that feels right for you.

Here's how it works:

1. Daily Practice: Each day, you'll find a powerful affirmation paired with a simple action step. Start your day by reading the affirmation out loud, allowing it to settle into your heart and mind.

2. Take Inspired Action: The action step will guide you in turning those words into reality. Think of it as planting seeds of change—small, intentional actions that add up to big transformations.

3. Flexibility is Key: Life is busy, and perfection is not the goal. If you miss a day or want to spend more time on a specific affirmation, that's okay. This is your journey, and you get to decide the pace.

4. Reflection and Gratitude: At the end of each week or chapter, take a moment to reflect. Write down how the affirmations have shifted your perspective or what actions brought you the most joy and clarity.

This book isn't about fixing you—because you are not broken. It's about awakening the joy, resilience, and power that's already within you. My hope is that as you move through these 365 days, you'll not only reclaim your joy but also discover the vibrant, unstoppable, and unapologetic person you were always meant to be.

Remember: joy isn't just something you feel—it's something you live. And I'm here to walk this journey with you.

With love, light, and endless joy,

Alesha Brown, The Joy Guru

Alesha Brown, The Joy Guru

CHAPTER I

RECLAIMING SELF-WORTH

REDISCOVER YOUR INHERENT VALUE AND EMBRACE SELF-LOVE.

"You alone are enough. You have nothing to prove to anybody."
— **Maya Angelou**

You are enough—just as you are. But how often do we forget this truth?

In a world that often measures worth by productivity, appearances, or accolades, it's easy to lose sight of our intrinsic value. This chapter is about coming home to yourself, peeling back the layers of self-doubt and external validation to rediscover the beauty of who you are.

Through these affirmations and actions, you'll begin the journey of rebuilding a foundation of self-love, reclaiming the power that comes with knowing your worth, and standing boldly in your truth.

DAY 1

**"I am worthy of joy, not because of what
I do, but because of who I am."**

I assure you, beloved, the essence of who you are
makes you **more** than <u>ENOUGH</u>!

Action Step: Write down three things you love
about yourself, unrelated to achievements, and
reflect on them daily this week.

DAY 2

"My value is not defined by others' opinions but by my inner truth."

Action Step: Journal about a time when you felt pressured by others' opinions and write how you'll choose differently next time.

DAY 3

"I release the need to compare my journey to anyone else's."

Action Step: Unfollow three social media accounts that make you feel less than and replace them with accounts that inspire joy and growth.

DAY 4

"Every day is a new opportunity to choose love and light for myself."

Action Step: Begin your morning with five minutes of meditation focused on gratitude for the day ahead.

DAY 5

"I deserve to occupy space boldly and unapologetically."

Action Step: Practice standing tall and making eye contact in every interaction today, even when it feels uncomfortable.

CHAPTER 2

BUILDING RESILIENCE FIRST STEPS

STRENGTHENING YOUR ABILITY TO FACE CHALLENGES WITH COURAGE AND GRACE

"Do not judge me by my success. Judge me by how many times I fell down and got back up again."

– Nelson Mandela

L ife can feel like a series of tests, but resilience is the skill that allows us to face each challenge and rise stronger on the other side. This chapter will guide you through the first steps of building resilience, reminding you of the strength you already possess and helping you cultivate it further.

Resilience isn't about avoiding struggle—it's about learning to navigate it with courage, adaptability, and unwavering self-belief. Through daily affirmations and actionable steps, you'll begin laying the groundwork for a life defined not by what happens to you but by how you rise.

DAY 6

"Challenges are my stepping stones to strength and wisdom."

Action Step: Reflect on one recent challenge and list three lessons it taught you.

1. _____
2. _____
3. _____

DAY 7

"I have the power to rewrite my narrative at any time."

Action Step: Write a paragraph describing the life you want and say it aloud every morning.

_____

_____

_____

_____

_____

_____

DAY 8

"I choose progress over perfection every single time."

Action Step: Identify one task you've been avoiding and take one small step toward completing it today.

CHAPTER 3

EMBRACING JOY

CHOOSING HAPPINESS IN THE PRESENT MOMENT

"Joy does not simply happen to us. We have to choose joy and keep choosing it every day."
– Henri J.M. Nouwen

J oy isn't something that happens to us; it's a choice we make every day. This chapter invites you to reconnect with the simple pleasures and profound moments of happiness already present in your life. Whether it's savoring the warmth of the sun, laughing with a loved one, or taking pride in your accomplishments, joy is always within reach.

Through these affirmations and actions, you'll learn to cultivate joy intentionally, even in the smallest of moments, and make it a guiding light in your daily life.

DAY 9

"Joy is my birthright, and I claim it with open arms."

Action Step: Do one thing today that brings you pure, childlike joy—whether it's dancing, singing, or playing a game.

DAY 10

"Happiness flows freely to me because I create space for it."

Action Step: Declutter one small area of your home today to make room for positive energy.

DAY 11

"My joy is a gift to the world, and I embrace it without apology."

Action Step: Share a moment of joy with someone else today—send a kind text, compliment someone, or give a small gift.

CHAPTER 4
PRACTICING MINDFULNESS
FINDING PEACE AND PRESENCE IN THE NOW

"Feelings come and go like clouds in a windy sky.
Conscious breathing is my anchor."
– Thich Nhat Hanh

In a world that pulls us in a thousand directions, mindfulness is the gift of being fully present in the moment. This chapter is about slowing down, grounding yourself, and connecting deeply to what's happening around you and within you.

Through affirmations and practices, you'll learn to quiet the noise, ease your mind, and anchor yourself in the calm and clarity that mindfulness brings. Whether you're new to mindfulness or looking to deepen your practice, these steps will guide you toward inner peace and a greater appreciation of life's simple moments.

DAY 12

"I anchor myself in the present moment, where peace resides."

Action Step: Spend five minutes observing your surroundings with your senses—notice sights, sounds, smells, and textures without judgment.

DAY 13

"I choose thoughts that nurture and uplift me."

Action Step: Write down one negative thought you've had recently and reframe it into a positive affirmation.

_____

_____

_____

_____

_____

_____

DAY 14

"Breathing deeply connects me to my inner calm."

Action Step: Practice a 4-7-8 breathing exercise: inhale for 4 seconds, hold for 7 seconds, and exhale for 8 seconds.

DAY 15

"Each moment of stillness restores my spirit."

Action Step: Set aside 10 minutes to sit quietly today, focusing on your breath or a calming image in your mind.

DAY 16

"I allow myself to slow down and savor life's simple pleasures."

Action Step: Enjoy one meal today without distractions—no TV, phone, or multitasking—focusing on each bite.

CHAPTER 5
HEALING AND FORGIVENESS
RELEASING THE PAST AND STEPPING INTO WHOLENESS

"Forgiveness is not an occasional act; it is a constant attitude."
– Martin Luther King Jr.

Healing is not about forgetting the wounds of the past—it's about learning to live fully despite them. Forgiveness is not just for others; it's a gift you give yourself, freeing your heart from the weight of resentment and pain. In this chapter, you'll embark on a journey of emotional and spiritual healing, learning to let go, embrace growth, and reclaim your wholeness. Through gentle affirmations and guided actions, you'll create space to heal and thrive.

DAY 17

"I forgive myself for past mistakes, knowing they were lessons."

Action Step: Write a letter of forgiveness to yourself for a regret you've been holding onto, and then shred or burn it as a release.

DAY 18

"I am healing one step at a time, and that is enough."

Action Step: Create a list of five self-care activities you can do this week and commit to doing at least one.

1. _____
2. _____
3. _____
4. _____
5. _____

DAY 19

"Forgiveness frees my heart to embrace love and joy."

Action Step: Identify someone you've been holding a grudge against and silently wish them peace and healing.

DAY 20

"I honor my pain as part of my growth."

Action Step: Journal about a painful experience and reflect on how it shaped your resilience or perspective.

_____

_____

_____

_____

_____

_____

_____

DAY 21

"I release what no longer serves me to make space for my highest good."

Action Step: Let go of one physical item, habit, or relationship that feels heavy or draining.

CHAPTER 6

EMPOWERMENT AND CONFIDENCE

OWNING YOUR POWER AND SHOWING UP FULLY

"No one can make you feel inferior without your consent."
– Eleanor Roosevelt

You are powerful, capable, and deserving of every good thing life has to offer. This chapter is about stepping into that truth with confidence and courage.

Through affirmations and intentional actions, you'll cultivate a deep belief in yourself and your abilities. It's time to shed self-doubt, silence the inner critic, and show up boldly in your life. You have what it takes, and this chapter will remind you of that every step of the way.

DAY 22

"I have the power to create the life I desire."

Action Step: Write down one specific goal you want to achieve and list three actionable steps to get closer to it. _____

1. _____
2. _____
3. _____

DAY 23

"I am capable of achieving greatness, one step at a time."

Action Step: Break a large task into smaller, manageable parts and complete the first part today.

DAY 24

"My voice matters, and I use it with confidence."

Action Step: Speak up in one situation today where you'd usually stay quiet, whether it's a meeting, conversation, or decision-making moment.

DAY 25

"I CELEBRATE MY UNIQUE GIFTS AND TALENTS."

Action Step: Write down three things you're good at and think of one way to use those gifts this week.

1. _____
2. _____
3. _____

DAY 26

"I AM BOLD, FEARLESS, AND UNSTOPPABLE."

Action Step: Do one thing today that pushes you out of your comfort zone, even if it's small.

CHAPTER 7
CULTIVATING GRATITUDE
TRANSFORMING YOUR PERSPECTIVE THROUGH THANKFULNESS

"Gratitude turns what we have into enough."
– Melody Beattie

Gratitude is the lens through which life becomes brighter, richer, and more meaningful. In this chapter, you'll learn to focus on the blessings already present in your life, no matter how small.

Gratitude isn't about ignoring challenges; it's about finding the good amidst them. These affirmations and actions will help you cultivate a daily practice of thankfulness that invites more abundance, joy, and connection into your life.

DAY 27

"Gratitude opens the door to unlimited blessings."

Action Step: Write a list of 10 things you're grateful for today, no matter how small.

1. _____
2. _____
3. _____
4. _____
5. _____
6. _____
7. _____
8. _____

9. _____

10. _____

DAY 28

"I find reasons to be thankful in every situation."

Action Step: Think of one challenge you've faced recently and identify at least one silver lining or lesson.

DAY 29

"Every breath I take is a reminder of life's abundance."

Action Step: Take a short walk outside and notice the abundance of nature around you.

DAY 30

"I radiate gratitude and attract more to be grateful for."

Action Step: Express gratitude to one person today with a heartfelt thank-you note or verbal acknowledgment.

DAY 31

"Appreciation for small moments creates a
joyful life."

Action Step: Pause to savor one small moment
today—a sip of coffee, a smile from a stranger, or
the warmth of the sun.

CHAPTER 8
STRENGTHENING BOUNDARIES
PROTECTING YOUR PEACE AND HONORING YOUR NEEDS

"Daring to set boundaries is about having the courage to love ourselves, even when we risk disappointing others."
– Brené Brown

Boundaries are not walls; they are bridges to healthier relationships and greater self-respect. This chapter is about recognizing your worth and learning to say "yes" to what serves you and "no" to what doesn't. Through affirmations and actionable steps, you'll gain clarity on your needs, honor your limits, and protect your peace. Strengthening boundaries isn't selfish—it's a necessary act of self-love.

DAY 32

"I honor my boundaries as an act of self-love."

Action Step: Identify one area where you need stronger boundaries and practice saying "no" with kindness today.

DAY 33

"My energy is sacred, and I protect it wisely."

Action Step: Write down three activities or people that drain your energy and decide to limit or eliminate one this week.

1. _____
2. _____
3. _____

DAY 34

"I have the right to say 'no' without guilt."

Action Step: Practice saying "no" in a mirror to grow comfortable asserting yourself.

DAY 35

"I surround myself with relationships that nurture and uplift me."

Action Step: Reach out to someone who makes you feel supported and schedule a time to connect.

DAY 36

"Setting boundaries allows me to show up fully and authentically."

Action Step: Write down one way a boundary has improved your life or could improve it.

_____

_____

CHAPTER 9
EMBRACING ABUNDANCE

INVITING PROSPERITY INTO EVERY AREA OF YOUR LIFE

"Abundance is not something we acquire. It is something we tune into."
– Wayne Dyer

Abundance is more than material wealth—it's a mindset that recognizes the limitless possibilities in life.

In this chapter, you'll learn to shift from scarcity thinking to an abundance mentality, celebrating the opportunities, blessings, and growth all around you. Through affirmations and actions, you'll open your heart and mind to receiving all that life has to offer.

DAY 37

"Abundance flows freely to me in all areas of my life."

Action Step: Write an abundance affirmation on a sticky note and place it where you'll see it daily.

DAY 38

"I release fear and welcome prosperity."

Action Step: List three things you desire and one small step you can take toward each goal.

1. _____
2. _____
3. _____

DAY 39

"I am a magnet for opportunities and success."

Action Step: Research or apply for one opportunity that aligns with your goals.

DAY 40

"My life is rich with blessings, seen and unseen."

Action Step: Create a gratitude jar and add one note about a blessing you experienced today.

DAY 41

"I open my heart and mind to receive all that is meant for me."

Action Step: Meditate for five minutes, repeating, "I am open to receiving."

CHAPTER 10

CELEBRATING JOY

MAKING HAPPINESS A DAILY RITUAL

"Find a place inside where there's joy, and the joy will burn out the pain."
– Joseph Campbell

J oy is not reserved for special occasions; it's something to celebrate every day. This chapter invites you to find and nurture the moments of happiness that bring life its sparkle. Through affirmations and actions, you'll discover how to make joy a daily habit, spreading positivity within yourself and to those around you.

DAY 42

"Joy is my choice, and I choose it every day."

Action Step: Do something today purely because it makes you happy, no matter how small.

DAY 43

"I find joy in the journey, not just the destination."

Action Step: Reflect on one goal you're pursuing and list three things you've enjoyed about the process.

1. _____

2. _____

3. _____

DAY 44

"My laughter is medicine for my soul."

Action Step: Watch a funny video or show or talk to someone who makes you laugh.

DAY 45

"I carry joy within me wherever I go."

Action Step: Smile at three people today and notice their reactions.

DAY 46

"I create moments of joy that sustain me."

Action Step: Schedule a "joy date" with yourself or loved ones—a time to do something you truly enjoy.

CHAPTER 11
UNLOCKING CREATIVITY
TAPPING INTO YOUR LIMITLESS IMAGINATION

"You can't use up creativity. The more you use, the more you have."
– Maya Angelou

You are a creative being, and your ideas and self-expression matter. This chapter is about unlocking your creative potential, experimenting without fear, and embracing the joy of creation. Through affirmations and actions, you'll reconnect with your inner artist, innovator, or dreamer, unleashing the limitless possibilities within you.

DAY 47

"My creativity flows effortlessly and inspires others."

Action Step: Try a creative activity today—drawing, writing, cooking, or anything that sparks your imagination.

DAY 48

"I am the author of my story, and I write it boldly."

Action Step: Write a short story or journal entry imagining your life five years from now.

_____

_____

_____

_____

_____

_____

_____

DAY 49

"I embrace curiosity and let it guide my creative journey."

Action Step: Learn something new today, like a word, skill, or fact, and see how it inspires you.

DAY 50

"My creativity is limitless and ever-expanding."

Action Step: Brainstorm 10 ideas for a passion project you'd like to explore.

1. _____
2. _____
3. _____
4. _____
5. _____
6. _____
7. _____
8. _____

9. _____

10. _____

DAY 51

"Every day is a canvas for me to paint my dreams."

Action Step: Create a vision board with images and words that represent your dreams.

CHAPTER 12

SUSTAINING JOY AND TRANSFORMATION

BUILDING A LASTING FOUNDATION FOR HAPPINESS AND GROWTH

"Happiness is not something ready-made. It comes from your own actions."
– Dalai Lama

Transformation is not a single moment; it's a continuous journey. Sustaining joy requires intention, commitment, and the willingness to adapt as you grow. This chapter will guide you in building practices that nurture long-term happiness and transformation. Through affirmations and actions, you'll learn how to maintain the positive changes you've cultivated, ensuring they become an enduring part of your life.

DAY 52

"I am joy, I give joy, I receive joy."

Action Step: Give someone an unexpected compliment or kind gesture today.

DAY 53

**"Transformation begins with the small choices
I make daily."**

Action Step: Reflect on one small habit you've
built and celebrate your progress.

DAY 54

"I am grateful for the person I am becoming."

Action Step: Write a letter to your future self, acknowledging how far you've come.

DAY 55

"Liberation is my birthright, and I embrace it fully."

Action Step: Do something that makes you feel free today, whether it's dancing, singing, or walking outside.

DAY 56

"My journey of joy and transformation is ongoing and beautiful."

Action Step: Look back on your affirmations and action steps from this year and note three areas of growth you're proud of.

1. _____
2. _____
3. _____

CHAPTER 13

LIVING WITH PURPOSE AND INTENTION

ALIGNING YOUR DAILY ACTIONS WITH YOUR DEEPEST VALUES

"The meaning of life is to find your gift. The purpose of life is to give it away."
– Pablo Picasso

When you live with purpose and intention, life feels richer, more meaningful, and deeply fulfilling. This chapter is about connecting with your "why" and ensuring your choices reflect the life you want to create. With each affirmation and action step, you'll clarify your values, strengthen your sense of direction, and find joy in living intentionally.

DAY 57

"I wake up each day with clarity and purpose."

Action Step: Write down your top three priorities for the day and focus on completing them.

1. _____
2. _____
3. _____

DAY 58

"I align my actions with my values."

Action Step: Reflect on your core values and identify one way you'll act in alignment with them today.

DAY 59

"I make intentional choices that nurture my growth."

Action Step: Choose one small habit to build or reinforce today that aligns with your long-term goals.

DAY 60

"I am present in each moment, and it is enough."

Action Step: Practice mindfulness by pausing three times today to take deep breaths and notice your surroundings.

DAY 61

"I am the creator of my life's masterpiece."

Action Step: Spend 15 minutes journaling about how you want your life to look and feel in five years.

_____

_____

_____

_____

_____

_____

_____

DAY 62

"I focus on what matters most to me."

Action Step: Write down the one thing that matters most to you and take a step toward nurturing it today.

DAY 63

"I release distractions and embrace focus."

Action Step: Turn off notifications and dedicate one hour to focused work or a meaningful activity.

DAY 64

"My actions today shape the future I desire."

Action Step: Choose one task you've been procrastinating on and commit to starting it today.

DAY 65

"I let go of what no longer serves my purpose."

Action Step: Declutter one area of your life—your workspace, your schedule, or even your thoughts.

DAY 66

"I trust my intuition to guide my decisions."

Action Step: Reflect on a decision you need to make and listen to your gut feelings about it.

DAY 67

"I choose progress over perfection."

Action Step: Start a task today without overthinking and focus on making progress, not perfecting it.

DAY 68

"My time and energy are sacred resources."

Action Step: Say "no" to one request or commitment that doesn't align with your priorities.

DAY 69

"I make space in my life for what truly matters."

Action Step: Plan a block of time today to spend with someone or doing something meaningful to you.

DAY 70

"I honor my purpose by living authentically."

Action Step: Identify one way you can show up as your true self in your interactions today.

DAY 71

"I create a life filled with meaning and joy."

Action Step: Do something today that aligns with both your passions and your purpose.

DAY 72

"I take inspired action toward my dreams."

Action Step: Identify one small action you can take today to move closer to your big goals.

DAY 73

"I let go of fear and embrace possibilities."

Action Step: Write down one fear holding you back and list two steps you can take to overcome it.

_____

1. _____
2. _____

DAY 74

"My life is a reflection of my highest values."

Action Step: Evaluate your schedule and remove one task or commitment that feels out of alignment.

DAY 75

"I wake up every day grateful for the gift of life."

Action Step: Start your morning by listing three things you're grateful for.

1. _____
2. _____
3. _____

DAY 76

"I invest my time and energy in what fuels my soul."

Action Step: Spend at least 30 minutes today doing something that brings you joy or peace.

DAY 77

"I am confident in my ability to live with purpose."

Action Step: Write a mantra for yourself about living purposefully and repeat it throughout the day.

_____

_____

_____

_____

_____

_____

DAY 78

"My dreams are valid and achievable."

Action Step: Create a list of your dreams and write one action step for each to start bringing them to fruition.

_____

_____

_____

_____

_____

_____

_____

DAY 79

"I am committed to becoming the best version of myself."

Action Step: Identify one area of personal growth and dedicate 15 minutes today to improving in that area.

DAY 80

"I give myself permission to pursue my passions fully."

Action Step: Take one step today to prioritize a passion project or creative endeavor.

CHAPTER 14

LIVING BOLDLY AND COURAGEOUSLY

STEPPING OUT OF YOUR COMFORT ZONE AND EMBRACING YOUR POWER

"Courage starts with showing up and letting ourselves be seen."
– Brené Brown

Courage isn't the absence of fear—it's choosing to act despite it. This chapter invites you to live boldly, take risks, and trust in your ability to thrive. Through affirmations and action steps, you'll learn to release hesitation, embrace your unique strengths, and show up confidently in every area of your life.

DAY 81

"I am brave enough to face my fears."

Action Step: Write down one fear that has held you back and take a small action toward overcoming it today.

DAY 82

"I embrace change as an opportunity for growth."

Action Step: Identify one recent change in your life and reflect on a positive outcome it has created.

DAY 83

"I step into my power with confidence and grace."

Action Step: Stand in front of a mirror, look into your eyes, and repeat today's affirmation with conviction.

DAY 84

"I trust myself to make bold decisions."

Action Step: Reflect on a decision you've been hesitant to make and take the first step toward resolving it.

DAY 85

"I let go of doubt and step boldly into my future."

Action Step: Write a list of reasons why you are capable of achieving your dreams.

_____

_____

_____

_____

_____

_____

_____

DAY 86

"I am fearless in pursuing my dreams."

Action Step: Take one bold action today toward a goal you've been delaying.

DAY 87

"I am worthy of taking up space and being heard."

Action Step: Speak up in a situation today where you would normally stay silent.

DAY 88

"I release hesitation and embrace confidence."

Action Step: Dress in an outfit today that makes you feel powerful and self-assured.

DAY 89

"I welcome challenges as opportunities to grow."

Action Step: Reframe one current challenge as a lesson and brainstorm a creative solution.

DAY 90

"I am unstoppable when I believe in myself."

Action Step: Reflect on a time when you achieved something you thought was impossible.

DAY 91

"I am courageous in the face of uncertainty."

Action Step: Identify one area of your life where you feel uncertain and take one small step toward clarity.

DAY 92

"I lead with courage and inspire others to do the same."

Action Step: Share an encouraging word or story of your bravery with someone today.

DAY 93

"I embrace risks that align with my highest goals."

Action Step: Write down one calculated risk you can take this week to advance a dream or project.

DAY 94

"I am resilient and bounce back stronger than before."

Action Step: Reflect on a setback and identify how you've grown or improved because of it.

DAY 95

"I celebrate the courage it takes to be myself."

Action Step: Do one thing today that expresses your authentic self unapologetically.

DAY 96

"I take bold steps toward my dreams every day."

Action Step: Set a specific, measurable goal and identify the next step you'll take to achieve it.

_____

_____

DAY 97

"I release fear and embrace freedom."

Action Step: Spend five minutes journaling about what freedom means to you and how you can create more of it in your life.

_____

_____

_____

_____

_____

_____

DAY 98

"I trust myself to handle whatever comes my way."

Action Step: List three personal strengths that help you face challenges with confidence.

1. _____
2. _____
3. _____

DAY 99

"I am bold enough to follow my intuition."

Action Step: Pause today when faced with a decision, and tune into your intuition before proceeding.

DAY 100

"I am worthy of my wildest dreams."

Action Step: Write down your biggest, most ambitious dream and brainstorm one small action to move closer to it.

DAY 101

"I am stronger than the doubts that try to hold me back."

Action Step: Identify one limiting belief you hold and write an affirmation to replace it.

DAY 102

"I face every challenge with courage and creativity."

Action Step: Approach a current challenge from a new perspective and brainstorm a unique solution.

DAY 103

"I take risks that align with my true purpose."

Action Step: Write down one action you've avoided out of fear and commit to taking it this week.

DAY 104

"I trust in my ability to overcome any obstacle."

Action Step: Reflect on an obstacle you've recently overcome and how it strengthened your belief in yourself.

DAY 105

"I am brave enough to try, even if I fail."

Action Step: Take one step today toward something you've been afraid to start, regardless of the outcome.

DAY 106

"I am proud of myself for showing up boldly each day."

Action Step: Write down three things you've done this week that demonstrate courage or boldness.

1. _____
2. _____
3. _____

DAY 107

"I live boldly, without apology."

Action Step: Take one action today that makes you feel bold and empowered.

CHAPTER 15

CULTIVATING GRATITUDE AND ABUNDANCE

RECOGNIZING THE BLESSINGS AROUND YOU AND INVITING MORE INTO YOUR LIFE.

"When you are grateful, fear disappears, and abundance appears."
– Tony Robbins

Gratitude and abundance go hand in hand. When you focus on what you have, rather than what you lack, you create space for more blessings to flow into your life.

This chapter will help you cultivate gratitude as a daily practice and shift your mindset to one of abundance. With affirmations and actions, you'll learn to celebrate life's gifts and attract even more of what you desire.

DAY 108

"Gratitude opens the door to limitless blessings."

Action Step: Write down five things you are grateful for today, no matter how small.

1. _____
2. _____
3. _____
4. _____
5. _____

DAY 109

"Abundance flows freely to me in every area of
my life."

Action Step: Reflect on one area of your life where
you feel abundant and celebrate it with a small
gesture.

DAY 110

"I focus on the good, and the good multiplies."

Action Step: Find one positive aspect of a difficult situation and write about it.

_____

_____

_____

_____

_____

_____

DAY III

"I am a magnet for joy, prosperity, and success."

Action Step: Spend five minutes visualizing your ideal life and feel gratitude for it as if it's already here.

DAY 112

"I appreciate the small blessings that make life beautiful."

Action Step: Take a walk and consciously notice five things in your environment that bring you joy or peace.

DAY 113

"I am grateful for the lessons that challenges bring."

Action Step: I am worthy of receiving life's abundance.

DAY 114

"I release lack and embrace abundance."

Action Step: Reflect on a scarcity mindset you've held and reframe it with an abundance perspective.

DAY 115

"I am surrounded by endless opportunities and possibilities."

Action Step: Brainstorm three new opportunities you could explore and commit to pursuing one.

1. _____
2. _____
3. _____

DAY 116

"My gratitude attracts even more to be grateful for."

Action Step: Send a thank-you note or message to someone who has positively impacted your life.

DAY 117

"I am grateful for the abundance that already exists in my life."

Action Step: Create a list of all the resources, relationships, and opportunities you currently have.

_____

_____

_____

_____

_____

_____

DAY 118

"I trust the universe to provide for me generously."

Action Step: Take one step today toward a goal you've been hesitant to pursue, trusting that support will come.

DAY 119

"I celebrate the success and abundance of others."

Action Step: Compliment or celebrate someone else's success today, genuinely and whole-heartedly.

DAY 120

"I am grateful for the lessons that challenges bring."

Action Step: Write about a challenge you've faced recently and the lesson or growth it offered.

_____

_____

_____

_____

_____

_____

_____

DAY 121

"Abundance comes easily when I am aligned
with my purpose."

Action Step: Identify one action that aligns with
your purpose and commit to doing it today.

DAY 122

"I am open to receiving unexpected blessings."

Action Step: Reflect on one unexpected blessing you've received in the past month and express gratitude for it.

DAY 123

"I am grateful for the journey as much as the destination."

Action Step: Write down three things you enjoy about the process of working toward a current goal.

1. _____
2. _____
3. _____

DAY 124

"I celebrate the abundance of love, joy, and wealth in my life."

Action Step: Do something today to celebrate a recent win or achievement, no matter how small.

DAY 125

.

"I release envy and embrace joy for others' success."

Action Step: Identify one person whose success inspires you and share your admiration with them.

DAY 126

"I choose to see abundance in every situation."

Action Step: Reframe a negative thought today by identifying something positive in the situation.

DAY 127

"I am abundant in health, wealth, and happiness."

Action Step: Take one action today that supports your physical, financial, or emotional well-being.

DAY 128

"I am grateful for the endless opportunities life offers."

Action Step: Seek out and say yes to one opportunity today that excites or challenges you.

DAY 129

"My gratitude creates a ripple effect of positivity."

Action Step: Share three things you're grateful for with someone close to you.

1. _____
2. _____
3. _____

DAY 130

"I trust that my needs are always met."

Action Step: Reflect on one time when life provided for you unexpectedly and express gratitude for it.

DAY 131

"Declutter one space in your home or work environment to make room for new energy and opportunities."

Action Step: Declutter one space in your home or work environment to make room for new energy and opportunities.

DAY 132

"I am deeply grateful for the gift of this moment."

Action Step: Spend five minutes practicing mindfulness, focusing on the sensations and feelings of the present.

DAY 133

"I create abundance through gratitude and action."

Action Step: Take one action step today toward manifesting something you're grateful for.

DAY 134

"Abundance is my natural state of being."

Action Step: Repeat today's affirmation three times aloud while looking at yourself in the mirror.

DAY 135

"I celebrate the limitless possibilities that lie before me."

Action Step: Write a list of 10 dreams or goals, no matter how big or small, and choose one to work toward today.

1. _____
2. _____
3. _____
4. _____
5. _____
6. _____
7. _____

8. _____
9. _____
10. _____

CHAPTER 16

EMBRACING HEALING AND WHOLENESS

RELEASING THE PAST AND RECLAIMING YOUR INNER STRENGTH

"The wound is the place where the light enters you."
– Rumi

Healing is a process of becoming whole again. It requires courage, patience, and self-compassion.

This chapter will guide you in letting go of pain, forgiving yourself and others, and creating space for new beginnings. Through affirmations and actions, you'll embrace the healing process and step into the fullness of who you are meant to be.

DAY 136

"I give myself permission to heal at my own pace."

Action Step: Reflect on an area where you need healing and write down one small step you can take toward it.

DAY 137

"I honor the process of healing, knowing it takes time."

Action Step: Spend 10 minutes journaling about what healing means to you and what it feels like.

DAY 138

"I am whole, even as I am healing."

Action Step: List three ways you are already whole and complete, despite any challenges.

1. _____
2. _____
3. _____

DAY 139

"I release the past and embrace the present with love."

Action Step: Write a forgiveness letter to yourself or someone else, even if you never send it.

DAY 140

"I nurture my mind, body, and spirit with compassion."

Action Step: Do one thing today that nourishes your mind (read), body (exercise), or spirit (meditate).

DAY 141

"I am patient with myself as I grow and heal."

Action Step: Identify one area where you've been hard on yourself and replace self-criticism with kindness.

DAY 142

"My pain is temporary, and my healing is eternal."

Action Step: Reflect on one painful experience and how it has shaped your growth or resilience.

DAY 143

"I release shame and embrace self-acceptance."

Action Step: Write down one thing you've felt ashamed of and reframe it as a learning experience.

_____

_____

_____

_____

_____

_____

DAY 144

"Healing is my birthright, and I claim it fully."

Action Step: Take 15 minutes today to practice a self-care ritual that makes you feel nurtured.

DAY 145

"I trust my body and mind to guide me toward healing."

Action Step: Listen to your body today—rest, hydrate, or stretch when you feel the need.

DAY 146

"I release what no longer serves me to make space for growth."

Action Step: Let go of one physical item, thought, or relationship that feels heavy or draining.

DAY 147

"I forgive myself for the mistakes of my past."

Action Step: Write a letter of forgiveness to yourself for something you regret, then let it go.

DAY 148

"I choose to focus on the lessons, not the wounds."

Action Step: Reflect on a challenging experience and write down three lessons it taught you.

DAY 149

"I deserve to be happy, healthy, and whole."

Action Step: Choose one habit that supports your happiness or health and commit to practicing it today.

DAY 150

"I release guilt and replace it with self-compassion."

Action Step: Write about a situation where you feel guilty and give yourself permission to move on.

DAY 151

"I am free from the chains of my past."

Action Step: Light a candle or hold a symbolic object while visualizing yourself letting go of a painful memory.

DAY 152

"I embrace all parts of myself with love and acceptance."

Action Step: Look in the mirror and say, "I love you" to yourself, focusing on your reflection.

DAY 153

"I am worthy of the healing I seek."

Action Step: Research one resource or support system that could help you on your healing journey.

DAY 154

"I let go of perfection and embrace progress."

Action Step: Identify one small win in your healing journey and celebrate it today.

DAY 155

"My scars are proof of my strength and resilience."

Action Step: Write about a "scar," physical or emotional, and how it represents your journey.

_____

_____

_____

_____

_____

_____

_____

DAY 156

"I open my heart to receive love and support."

Action Step: Reach out to someone you trust and share what you're feeling or experiencing.

DAY 157

"I am grateful for the lessons that challenges bring."

Action Step: Write a gratitude list specifically for the progress you've made in healing.

DAY 158

"I am gentle with myself as I let go of old wounds."

Action Step: Spend five minutes meditating or practicing deep breathing to soothe your mind.

DAY 159

"I allow joy to replace pain in my heart."

Action Step: Do one thing today that brings you pure, unfiltered joy, no matter how small.

DAY 160

"I create a safe space for my healing to unfold."

Action Step: Dedicate a corner of your home to your healing journey, filling it with items that bring you peace.

DAY 161

"I trust the timing of my healing."

Action Step: Reflect on one area where you've been impatient with yourself and release the need to rush.

DAY 162

"I am free to live fully and joyfully."

Action Step: Do something today that makes you feel alive—dance, sing, or take a spontaneous walk.

CHAPTER 17
NURTURING INNER PEACE AND BALANCE

CREATING HARMONY IN YOUR MIND, BODY, AND SPIRIT

"Peace comes from within. Do not seek it without."
– Buddha

Inner peace isn't about eliminating life's chaos; it's about finding calm amidst it. Balance comes from aligning your priorities with your values and making space for rest, joy, and growth. This chapter will help you nurture peace and harmony in your life through affirmations and actions that ground you in the present moment.

DAY 163

"I am at peace with where I am in life."

Action Step: Spend five minutes reflecting on what you appreciate about your current circumstances.

DAY 164

"I choose peace over worry in every situation."

Action Step: Write down one worry and replace it with a calming affirmation.

_____

_____

DAY 165

"I create balance in my life by prioritizing what matters most."

Action Step: Identify one area where you feel unbalanced and take a small step to restore harmony.

DAY 166

"My inner peace is unshakable, no matter what happens around me."

Action Step: Take 10 minutes for a calming activity, such as meditation, deep breathing, or gentle stretching.

DAY 167

"I release the need to control everything and trust the process."

Action Step: Reflect on a situation you cannot control and consciously let go of your attachment to its outcome.

DAY 168

"I protect my peace by setting healthy boundaries."

Action Step: Identify one boundary you need to enforce and take a step to honor it today.

DAY 169

"I find stillness within me, even in chaos."

Action Step: Practice grounding yourself by focusing on five things you can see, hear, or touch in your surroundings.

DAY 170

"I choose kindness and calm in all my interactions."

Action Step: Approach a conversation today with intentional kindness, even if it's challenging.

DAY 171

"I align my life with the rhythm of peace and balance."

Action Step: Spend 10 minutes journaling about what peace and balance look like for you.

DAY 172

"I let go of what disrupts my peace and embrace tranquility."

Action Step: Declutter one physical or emotional area of your life today.

DAY 173

"I am calm, centered, and grounded in this moment."

Action Step: Sit quietly with your feet flat on the ground and focus on your breath for five minutes.

DAY 174

"I make space for rest and rejuvenation."

Action Step: Schedule time today to rest without guilt—whether it's a nap, reading, or simply sitting quietly.

DAY 175

"I flow effortlessly through life's ups and downs."

Action Step: Reflect on a recent challenge and write about how you navigated it with grace.

DAY 176

"I release tension and invite calm into my mind and body."

Action Step: Try a progressive muscle relaxation exercise to release tension from head to toe.

DAY 177

"I create harmony in my relationships through open communication."

Action Step: Reach out to someone with whom you want to strengthen your connection and have a meaningful conversation.

DAY 178

"I embrace balance in my work, relationships, and self-care."

Action Step: Reflect on how you've been balancing these areas and adjust your schedule if needed.

DAY 179

"I find peace in accepting life as it is."

Action Step: Write about one area of life you've resisted accepting and how you can release that resistance.

_____

_____

_____

_____

_____

_____

DAY 180

"I trust in the flow of life to guide me to peace."

Action Step: Take a slow, mindful walk today and focus on the natural flow of your breath and movement.

DAY 181

"My peace comes from within, not from external circumstances."

Action Step: Write a list of five activities or thoughts that bring you inner peace and do one today.

1. _____
2. _____
3. _____
4. _____
5. _____

DAY 182

"I embrace serenity by letting go of negativity."

Action Step: Identify one negative thought or belief and replace it with a positive affirmation.

DAY 183

"I honor my need for quiet and stillness."

Action Step: Dedicate 15 minutes today to silence —no phone, TV, or distractions—just quiet reflection.

DAY 184

"I bring peace to the world by being at peace within myself."

Action Step: Perform one act of kindness today to share your calm energy with someone else.

DAY 185

"I choose patience and calm when faced with challenges."

Action Step: When faced with stress today, pause, take three deep breaths, and approach the situation calmly.

DAY 186

"I am in control of how I respond to life."

Action Step: Reflect on a time when you responded calmly to a situation and how it benefited you.

DAY 187

"I create peace by focusing on solutions, not problems."

Action Step: Write down a current problem and brainstorm three possible solutions.

1. ——————————————————————
2. ——————————————————————
3. ——————————————————————

DAY 188

"I cultivate peace through gratitude."

Action Step: List three peaceful moments from your day and reflect on why they brought you joy.

1. _____
2. _____
3. _____

DAY 189

"I live in harmony with my inner and outer worlds."

Action Step: Spend five minutes aligning your physical environment (e.g., tidying up a room) to reflect inner calm.

DAY 190

"I am grateful for the peace I am building in my life."

Action Step: Write a gratitude list focusing on the moments of calm and balance you've experienced recently.

_____

_____

_____

_____

_____

_____

CHAPTER 18

STRENGTHENING RESILIENCE AND DETERMINATION

BUILDING THE STRENGTH TO PERSEVERE AND THRIVE

"She stood in the storm, and when the wind did not blow her way, she adjusted her sails."
– Elizabeth Edwards

Resilience is the ability to rise, again and again, no matter how many times life knocks you down. Determination keeps you moving forward, even when the path feels unclear. This chapter is about strengthening your inner resolve through affirmations and actions that remind you of your strength, courage, and ability to overcome any challenge.

DAY 191

"I am resilient and capable of overcoming any challenge."

Action Step: Write down one recent challenge and list three strengths you used to navigate it.

_____

1. _____
2. _____
3. _____

DAY 192

"I grow stronger with every setback I face."

Action Step: Reflect on a moment when you overcame adversity and how it shaped you.

DAY 193

"I trust my ability to persevere in the face of difficulties."

Action Step: Identify a goal you've been struggling with and take one small action to move forward.

DAY 194

"I rise above obstacles with courage and grace."

Action Step: Think of one challenge you're currently facing and write down a positive reframe or lesson from it.

_____

_____

_____

_____

_____

_____

DAY 195

"I have everything I need within me to succeed."

Action Step: List three resources, skills, or qualities you possess that support your goals.

1. —————————————————————
2. —————————————————————
3. —————————————————————

DAY 196

"I am unstoppable when I focus on my dreams."

Action Step: Set aside 15 minutes today to work on a dream or goal, even if it's just planning.

DAY 197

"I am stronger than any doubt or fear."

Action Step: Write down one fear or doubt and create an action plan to overcome it.

_____

_____

_____

_____

_____

_____

DAY 198

"I embrace challenges as opportunities to grow."

Action Step: Identify a current challenge and brainstorm three ways it can help you grow.

_____

1. _____
2. _____
3. _____

DAY 199

"I trust the process of my journey, even when it feels difficult."

Action Step: Reflect on a time when patience and persistence paid off, and apply that lesson to today.

DAY 200

"My determination fuels my success."

Action Step: Write down one big goal and three steps you can take to stay committed to achieving it. _____

1. _____
2. _____
3. _____

DAY 201

"I am resilient and bounce back stronger every time."

Action Step: Recall a moment when you recovered from a setback and celebrate your resilience.

DAY 202

"I am proud of my ability to keep going."

Action Step: Write a note of encouragement to yourself for when you face tough times.

_____

_____

_____

_____

_____

_____

_____

DAY 203

"I face challenges with confidence and creativity."

Action Step: Think of a current issue and approach it from a fresh, creative perspective.

DAY 204

"I am capable of achieving anything I set my mind to."

Action Step: Choose one long-term goal and write a list of the steps you've already completed toward it.

_____

_____

_____

_____

_____

_____

_____

DAY 205

"I am strong, determined, and focused on my path."

Action Step: Eliminate one distraction today that takes you away from your priorities.

DAY 206

"I let go of the past and focus on my future."

Action Step: Write down one regret or disappointment and release it by tearing or shredding the paper.

DAY 207

"I turn obstacles into stepping stones for success."

Action Step: Identify one obstacle in your path and brainstorm a way to use it to your advantage.

DAY 208

"I am courageous in pursuing my dreams."

Action Step: Take one bold action today that moves you closer to a personal or professional dream.

DAY 209

"I am unshaken by doubt because I believe in myself."

Action Step: Write down three affirmations about your strengths and repeat them throughout the day.

1. _____

2. _____

3. _____

DAY 210

"I focus on progress, not perfection."

Action Step: Choose one task and commit to completing it, even if it's not perfect.

DAY 211

"I am patient with myself as I build my future."

Action Step: Reflect on a big goal and list three small, actionable steps you can take today.

1. _____
2. _____
3. _____

DAY 212

"I bounce back quickly and powerfully."

Action Step: Reflect on a setback that initially felt overwhelming and how you overcame it.

DAY 213

"I trust my resilience to carry me through any storm."

Action Step: Spend five minutes visualizing yourself successfully overcoming a current challenge.

DAY 214

"I am determined to succeed, no matter how long it takes."

Action Step: Write down a goal you've been pursuing for a long time and recommit to it today.

DAY 215

"My perseverance is my greatest strength."

Action Step: Identify one task you've been avoiding and commit to completing it today.

DAY 216

"I trust that I am on the right path, even if I can't see the destination."

Action Step: Take a moment to appreciate the progress you've made, even if it feels small.

DAY 217

"I am capable of adapting to any challenge."

Action Step: Think of a situation where adaptability helped you and apply that mindset to a current issue.

DAY 218

"I believe in my ability to overcome and achieve."

Action Step: Write down a motivational mantra for yourself and repeat it every morning this week.

_____

_____

_____

_____

_____

_____

_____

DAY 219

"I am resilient, determined, and unstoppable."

Action Step: Reflect on three moments in your life when resilience helped you succeed, and draw strength from them today.

1. _____
2. _____
3. _____

DAY 220

"I am proud of how far I've come and excited for what lies ahead."

Action Step: Write a letter to your future self, celebrating your resilience and outlining your dreams.

CHAPTER 19
UNLOCKING CREATIVITY AND SELF-EXPRESSION

TAPPING INTO YOUR UNIQUE GIFTS AND EXPRESSING YOUR AUTHENTIC SELF

"The world always seems brighter when you've just made something that wasn't there before."
– Neil Gaiman

Creativity is your birthright. It's not about perfection—it's about exploring, experimenting, and expressing who you are. This chapter will guide you in embracing your creativity and finding joy in the process of making and doing. Through affirmations and actions, you'll reconnect with your imagination, confidence, and the beauty of self-expression.

DAY 221

"I am a creative being, and my ideas have value."

Action Step: Spend 10 minutes brainstorming or doodling ideas for a project or hobby that excites you.

DAY 222

"My creativity flows freely and effortlessly."

Action Step: Set aside time today to try a creative activity you enjoy, such as writing, drawing, or cooking.

DAY 223

"I express myself authentically through my creativity."

Action Step: Create something today that feels like a true reflection of who you are.

DAY 224

"I give myself permission to explore new ideas and possibilities."

Action Step: Try a new activity or learn something today that sparks your curiosity.

DAY 225

"I am inspired by the world around me."

Action Step: Take a walk or spend time in nature and jot down or sketch what inspires you.

DAY 226

"I create without judgment or fear of imperfection."

Action Step: Start a creative project today without worrying about the outcome—just enjoy the process.

DAY 227

"My creativity is a gift I share with the world."

Action Step: Share something you've created with someone who would appreciate it.

DAY 228

"I am open to inspiration in all its forms."

Action Step: Watch, read, or listen to something new that challenges or excites your imagination.

DAY 229

"I transform my ideas into reality with ease."

Action Step: Choose one creative idea you've been putting off and take the first step toward bringing it to life.

DAY 230

"I embrace my unique creative voice."

Action Step: Reflect on what makes your perspective or ideas unique and write them down.

DAY 231

"I approach challenges with creativity and innovation."

Action Step: Think of a current problem and brainstorm three creative solutions.

DAY 232

"I am playful and curious in my creative pursuits."

Action Step: Try a fun, low-stakes creative activity today, like coloring or building something with your hands.

DAY 233

"My creativity connects me to my inner joy."

Action Step: Dedicate 15 minutes today to a creative activity that brings you pure happiness.

DAY 234

"I am confident in my ability to create something meaningful."

Action Step: Start a project today that feels meaningful, even if it's just the planning phase.

DAY 235

"I am inspired by my past experiences and future dreams."

Action Step: Reflect on a memory or dream that inspires you, and create something based on it.

DAY 236

"I nurture my creativity with time, patience, and love."

Action Step: Block out 30 minutes this week to focus solely on a creative project or idea.

DAY 237

"I am surrounded by endless sources of inspiration."

Action Step: Visit a new place—a park, museum, or even a new coffee shop—and observe how it inspires you.

DAY 238

"I express myself fearlessly and authentically."

Action Step: Write or speak openly about something that matters deeply to you.

DAY 239

"I create beauty and meaning in the world."

Action Step: Think of a way to add beauty or meaning to your day—a handwritten note, a small gift, or an act of kindness.

DAY 240

"I allow myself to be creative in ways that feel good to me."

Action Step: Reflect on your favorite creative activities and schedule time to enjoy one of them this week.

DAY 241

"My creativity grows stronger with each step I take."

Action Step: Commit to spending five minutes daily on a creative project for the next week.

DAY 242

"I let go of creative blocks and trust in my flow."

Action Step: Identify one thing that feels like a creative block and take a small step to work through it.

DAY 243

"I am proud of my creativity and the joy it brings me."

Action Step: Share your creative process or result with someone you trust and celebrate your efforts.

DAY 244

"I celebrate the creativity in myself and others."

Action Step: Compliment or encourage someone else's creative work today.

DAY 245

"I express my feelings through my creative outlets."

Action Step: Use art, writing, or another medium to express how you feel today.

DAY 246

"I am free to create without limits or expectations."

Action Step: Spend 15 minutes on a project where the outcome doesn't matter—just enjoy the act of creating.

DAY 247

"My creativity is ever-expanding and limitless."

Action Step: Reflect on a creative goal you've accomplished and imagine what's next.

DAY 248

"I am grateful for my creative energy and vision."

Action Step: Write down three things you love about your creative spirit or abilities.

1. _____
2. _____
3. _____

DAY 249

"I am bold in my self-expression and creativity."

Action Step: Do something today that feels bold or daring, creatively or otherwise.

DAY 250

"My creativity connects me to the world in meaningful ways."

Action Step: Share a creative idea or vision with someone and invite their perspective or collaboration.

CHAPTER 20
EMBODYING CONFIDENCE AND SELF-EMPOWERMENT

STANDING TALL IN YOUR POWER AND BELIEVING IN YOUR WORTH

"With realization of one's own potential and self-confidence in one's ability, one can build a better world."
– Dalai Lama

Confidence is not something you wait for —it's something you build by trusting yourself and stepping boldly into your life. This chapter will help you cultivate unshakable self-belief and embody your power through affirmations and intentional actions. You are worthy, capable, and deserving of every success and joy life has to offer.

DAY 251

"I am confident in who I am and what I bring to the world."

Action Step: Write down three things that make you unique and valuable.

1. _____
2. _____
3. _____

DAY 252

"I trust myself to make decisions that align
with my values."

Action Step: Reflect on a decision you need to
make and choose based on what feels authentic
to you.

DAY 253

"I embrace my strengths and use them to empower others."

Action Step: Identify one of your strengths and think of how you can use it to help someone today.

DAY 254

"I show up boldly and unapologetically in all areas of my life."

Action Step: Speak up in a situation today where you'd normally stay silent.

DAY 255

"I am worthy of every success and opportunity that comes my way."

Action Step: Write down one goal you've achieved and reflect on why you deserve your success.

_____

_____

_____

DAY 256

"I release self-doubt and replace it with self-belief."

Action Step: Write down a self-limiting belief and reframe it as an empowering statement.

DAY 257

"I am a leader in my own life and inspire others to lead theirs."

Action Step: Take charge of one area of your life today by setting a clear intention or plan.

DAY 258

"I celebrate my achievements and take pride in my progress."

Action Step: List three accomplishments, big or small, that you're proud of this week.

1. _____

2. _____

3. _____

DAY 259

"I am capable of handling anything that comes my way."

Action Step: Recall a past situation where you handled a challenge with confidence and re-silience.

DAY 260

"I am deserving of love, success, and happiness."

Action Step: Write down a list of things you love about yourself and read it aloud.

_____

_____

_____

_____

_____

_____

DAY 261

"I attract opportunities that align with my purpose and vision."

Action Step: Research or apply for one opportunity today that excites or aligns with your goals.

DAY 262

"I am courageous in pursuing my dreams."

Action Step: Take one bold action today toward a personal or professional dream.

DAY 263

"I trust my abilities to create the life I desire."

Action Step: Write down a long-term goal and list three strengths that will help you achieve it.

1. _____
2. _____
3. _____

DAY 264

"I radiate confidence and positivity in everything I do."

Action Step: Pay attention to your posture and body language today—stand tall and smile.

DAY 265

"I honor my journey and trust in my path."

Action Step: Reflect on how far you've come and write a note of gratitude to your past self.

DAY 266

"I am worthy of taking up space and being seen."

Action Step: Walk into a room today with your head held high, making eye contact with those around you.

DAY 267

"I embrace my imperfections and love myself fully."

Action Step: Write down one thing you've been critical of yourself for and reframe it as a positive trait.

_____

_____

_____

_____

_____

_____

_____

DAY 268

"I am a magnet for success and abundance."

Action Step: Visualize yourself achieving a big goal and feel the joy and excitement as if it's already done.

DAY 269

"I give myself permission to succeed and thrive."

Action Step: Set aside time today to focus on a project or goal that feels meaningful to you.

DAY 270

"I exude confidence in my words, actions, and presence."

Action Step: Practice speaking clearly and confidently in one interaction today.

DAY 271

"I am in control of my thoughts, choices, and actions."

Action Step: Take a moment to pause and choose your response in a situation that challenges you today.

DAY 272

"I release the need for approval and trust in my own worth."

Action Step: Reflect on an area where you've sought external validation and affirm your self-worth instead.

DAY 273

"I am resilient and rise stronger from every setback."

Action Step: Write down one lesson you've learned from a recent failure or disappointment.

_____

_____

_____

DAY 274

"I am a powerful force for good in the world."

Action Step: Perform one small act of kindness today that makes an impact on someone else.

DAY 275

"I honor my voice and speak my truth fearlessly."

Action Step: Share your thoughts or feelings with someone openly and honestly today.

DAY 276

"I am proud of the person I am becoming."

Action Step: Write a letter to your future self, describing the confident and empowered person you are becoming.

DAY 277

"I trust that I am exactly where I need to be."

Action Step: Reflect on your current season of life and list three things you appreciate about it.

DAY 278

"I deserve every blessing that comes my way."

Action Step: Write down one recent blessing or opportunity and express gratitude for it.

_____

_____

DAY 279

"I create the life I desire through my confidence and determination."

Action Step: Take one actionable step today that moves you closer to a major goal.

DAY 280

"I am enough, exactly as I am."

Action Step: Look at yourself in the mirror and repeat today's affirmation with conviction.

CHAPTER 21

CELEBRATING JOY AND BUILDING POSITIVITY

CREATING A LIFE FILLED WITH HAPPINESS AND OPTIMISM

*"Keep your face always toward the sunshine—
and shadows will fall behind you."*
– Walt Whitman

J oy and positivity aren't reserved for perfect moments—they can be cultivated every day. This chapter is about celebrating life's wins, both big and small, and creating a mindset that seeks out the good in every situation. Through affirmations and actions, you'll build a life where joy becomes a natural and constant presence.

DAY 281

"Joy is my natural state, and I choose it daily."

Action Step: List three things that bring you joy and make time for one of them today.

1. _____
2. _____
3. _____

DAY 282

"I welcome positivity and happiness into my life."

Action Step: Begin your day by writing down one positive intention for the day ahead.

DAY 283

"I am a source of joy and light for those around me."

Action Step: Share a kind word or compliment with someone today to brighten their day.

DAY 284

"I find joy in the small moments of everyday life."

Action Step: Pause to savor a simple pleasure today, such as a cup of coffee or the sound of laughter.

DAY 285

"I create my own happiness through my choices and actions."

Action Step: Reflect on a choice you made recently that brought you happiness and celebrate it.

DAY 286

"I am surrounded by people and experiences that bring me joy."

Action Step: Reach out to someone who uplifts you and spend time connecting with them.

DAY 287

"I focus on the good and let go of negativity."

Action Step: Write down one negative thought and replace it with a positive one.

DAY 288

"My heart is full of gratitude and joy."

Action Step: Reflect on three things you're grateful for today and smile as you think about them.

1. _____
2. _____
3. _____

DAY 289

"I allow myself to feel pure, unfiltered happiness."

Action Step: Do something spontaneous and fun today that makes you feel like a kid again.

DAY 290

"I radiate joy and positivity in every interaction."

Action Step: Approach all your interactions today with a positive attitude and a genuine smile.

DAY 291

"I release stress and embrace calm, joyful energy."

Action Step: Spend 10 minutes doing a relaxation exercise, such as yoga, meditation, or deep breathing.

DAY 292

"I am grateful for the abundance of joy in my life."

Action Step: Write a gratitude letter to someone who has brought joy into your life and share it with them.

DAY 293

"I choose to see the bright side of every situation."

Action Step: Reflect on a recent challenge and identify one positive aspect or lesson it brought you.

DAY 294

"I am worthy of living a joyful and fulfilling life."

Action Step: Spend time today doing something that feels meaningful and fulfilling to you.

DAY 295

"I let go of worry and welcome peace and happiness."

Action Step: Write down one worry and consciously release it, trusting that everything will work out.

DAY 296

"I celebrate my life and the people in it."

Action Step: Plan a small celebration or gesture to appreciate someone important in your life.

DAY 297

"Joy flows to me effortlessly and abundantly."

Action Step: Practice affirmations for five minutes, repeating this one aloud with a smile.

DAY 298

"I bring positivity to every space I enter."

Action Step: Walk into a room today with an intentional positive energy and notice how it affects others.

DAY 299

"I attract happiness through my thoughts and actions."

Action Step: Spend time visualizing your happiest moments and the feelings they brought you.

DAY 300

"I am a beacon of hope, joy, and positivity."

Action Step: Share a message of hope or encouragement with someone who may need it today.

DAY 301

"I embrace the beauty and joy of the present moment."

Action Step: Spend five minutes observing your surroundings and finding joy in what you see, hear, or feel.

DAY 302

"I create space for joy in my daily life."

Action Step: Schedule 30 minutes today to do something that sparks joy and refreshes your spirit.

DAY 303

"I surround myself with uplifting and inspiring energy."

Action Step: Spend time with people, music, or activities that boost your mood and energy.

DAY 304

"I honor the joy in others as well as in myself."

Action Step: Ask someone about a recent happy moment in their life and share in their joy.

DAY 305

"I live my life with a spirit of gratitude and happiness."

Action Step: At the end of the day, reflect on one moment that brought you joy and write about it.

DAY 306

"I spread positivity and joy wherever I go."

Action Step: Compliment or encourage at least three people today.

DAY 307

"I am grateful for the joy I give and receive."

Action Step: Think of a way you've brought joy to someone else recently, and celebrate that act of kindness.

DAY 308

"I find happiness in giving as well as receiving."

Action Step: Perform one small act of kindness for someone today.

DAY 309

"I am grateful for the limitless potential for joy in my life."

Action Step: Write down three new experiences or goals that would bring you joy and consider pursuing one.

1. _____
2. _____
3. _____

DAY 310

"I am the creator of my joy-filled life."

Action Step: Reflect on how you've created joyful moments in your life and how you can create more.

CHAPTER 22

MANIFESTING DREAMS AND PURPOSE

TURNING YOUR VISION INTO REALITY THROUGH FOCUSED INTENTION

"Go confidently in the direction of your dreams. Live the life you have imagined."
– Henry David Thoreau

Your dreams are valid, and your purpose is powerful. Manifestation begins when you align your thoughts, actions, and energy with what you truly desire.

This chapter will guide you in clarifying your goals, taking inspired steps toward them, and trusting the process. Through affirmations and actions, you'll transform your dreams into a reality that reflects your highest vision.

DAY 321

"I AM WORTHY OF ACHIEVING MY DREAMS."

Action Step: Write down one dream you have and list three steps you can take toward it today.

1. _____
2. _____
3. _____

DAY 312

"I align my actions with my vision for the future."

Action Step: Review your daily activities and identify one way to align them more closely with your long-term goals.

DAY 313

"I am focused and determined to bring my
dreams to life."

Action Step: Spend 20 minutes today working
uninterrupted on a task related to your dreams.

DAY 314

"I trust that my purpose is unfolding perfectly."

Action Step: Reflect on your purpose and write a paragraph about how it's showing up in your life.

DAY 315

"I have the power to create the life I desire."

Action Step: Visualize your ideal life for five minutes, focusing on how it feels and looks.

DAY 316

"I take consistent action toward my goals every day."

Action Step: Choose one small goal and take the next actionable step toward achieving it today.

DAY 317

"I am open to receiving the opportunities
meant for me."

Action Step: Say yes to one new opportunity that
aligns with your goals or interests today.

DAY 318

"I manifest my dreams by believing in them fully."

Action Step: Write a letter to yourself describing how it will feel to achieve one of your biggest dreams.

DAY 319

"I release fear and replace it with faith in my journey."

Action Step: Reflect on one fear holding you back and list two reasons why it doesn't define you.

DAY 320

"I am surrounded by people and resources that support my purpose."

Action Step: Reach out to someone in your network who inspires or supports you.

DAY 321

"I welcome success and abundance into my life."

Action Step: Write down three ways you define success and take one small step toward achieving it.

1. _____
2. _____
3. _____

DAY 322

"I trust the timing of my dreams coming true."

Action Step: Reflect on an area where you've been impatient and write about how you can cultivate trust instead.

_____

_____

_____

_____

_____

_____

_____

DAY 323

"I am the author of my story and write it boldly."

Action Step: Journal about how you want the next chapter of your life to look and feel.

_____

_____

_____

_____

_____

_____

DAY 324

"I attract opportunities that align with my purpose."

Action Step: Spend 10 minutes today researching or applying for opportunities that excite you.

DAY 325

"I release self-doubt and embrace confidence in my abilities."

Action Step: Write down three affirmations about your capabilities and repeat them aloud.

1. _____
2. _____
3. _____

DAY 326

"I am grateful for the progress I am making."

Action Step: Reflect on a recent accomplishment and express gratitude for your hard work and growth.

DAY 327

"I am clear about what I want and how to achieve it."

Action Step: Write down one specific goal and create a timeline for completing it.

_____

_____

_____

_____

_____

_____

_____

DAY 328

"I take responsibility for creating my dream life."

Action Step: Identify one area where you've been holding back and commit to taking action today.

DAY 329

"I trust in my ability to navigate obstacles on my path."

Action Step: Reflect on a recent challenge and identify how it's preparing you for greater success.

DAY 330

"I celebrate every small victory on my journey."

Action Step: Choose one small win from today or this week and celebrate it in a meaningful way.

DAY 331

"I embrace change as a natural part of achieving my dreams."

Action Step: Reflect on a change you're experiencing and list three ways it benefits your growth.

DAY 332

"I act boldly in the direction of my purpose."

Action Step: Take a bold action today that moves you closer to a big goal.

DAY 333

"I trust that the universe is working in my favor."

Action Step: Write a gratitude list of three unexpected blessings or opportunities you've received.

1. _____
2. _____
3. _____

DAY 334

"I have the courage to dream big and pursue my vision."

Action Step: Write down one "big" dream that excites you and commit to exploring how to make it happen.

DAY 335

"I let go of what no longer serves me to make space for my dreams."

Action Step: Release one habit, belief, or item that feels like it's holding you back.

DAY 336

"I am grateful for the clarity I have about my purpose."

Action Step: Spend 10 minutes meditating or journaling about your purpose and what it means to you.

DAY 337

"I align my daily actions with my highest vision."

Action Step: Write down one action you can take today to align your actions with your vision.

DAY 338

"I celebrate the journey of growth and transformation."

Action Step: Reflect on three ways you've grown in the past year and how it's brought you closer to your dreams.

1. _____
2. _____
3. _____

DAY 339

"I MANIFEST GREATNESS THROUGH FOCUS AND DEDICATION."

Action Step: Spend 20 minutes today working on something that aligns with your dreams and purpose.

DAY 340

"I am grateful for the life I am creating."

Action Step: Write a gratitude letter to your future self, thanking yourself for your courage and hard work.

CHAPTER 23

PRACTICING SELF-COMPASSION AND LOVE

LOVING YOURSELF THROUGH EVERY STAGE OF THE JOURNEY

"You yourself, as much as anybody in the entire universe, deserve your love and affection."
– Buddha

Self-compassion is the foundation of joy, resilience, and transformation. It's about treating yourself with the same kindness you'd offer a dear friend.

This chapter invites you to cultivate unconditional self-love, embrace your imperfections, and honor your progress. Through affirmations and actions, you'll learn to nurture yourself and create a lasting relationship of care and kindness with your inner self.

DAY 341

"I am worthy of my own love and care."

Action Step: Write down three ways you can show yourself love today and commit to doing at least one.

1. _____
2. _____
3. _____

DAY 342

"I treat myself with kindness and understanding."

Action Step: Reflect on a recent mistake or shortcoming and write a note of forgiveness to yourself.

DAY 343

"I am patient with myself as I grow and evolve."

Action Step: Identify one area where you've been hard on yourself and commit to practicing patience instead.

DAY 344

"I embrace my imperfections as part of my beauty."

Action Step: Write down one "flaw" you've been critical of and reframe it as a strength or unique trait.

DAY 345

"I speak to myself with love and encouragement."

Action Step: Write three positive affirmations about yourself and say them aloud in front of a mirror.

1. _____
2. _____
3. _____

DAY 346

"I honor my needs and take care of myself fully."

Action Step: Check in with yourself today—mentally, physically, and emotionally—and meet one unmet need.

DAY 347

"I deserve rest and rejuvenation."

Action Step: Schedule time today to rest or do something that refreshes your mind and body.

DAY 348

"I release guilt and replace it with self-acceptance."

Action Step: Write down one thing you've felt guilty about and release it by affirming your intentions were good.

DAY 349

"I celebrate who I am in this moment."

Action Step: List three qualities or achievements about yourself that you are proud of today.

1. _____
2. _____
3. _____

DAY 350

"I nurture my mind, body, and spirit with love and care."

Action Step: Dedicate 30 minutes to an activity that nourishes one of these areas.

DAY 351

"I deserve love and acceptance, just as I am."

Action Step: Write a love letter to yourself, affirming your worth and beauty.

DAY 352

"I am gentle with myself when I feel
overwhelmed."

Action Step: Take 10 minutes to pause and
breathe deeply when feeling stressed today.

DAY 353

"I release the pressure to be perfect."

Action Step: Identify one area where you've been striving for perfection and allow yourself to simply do your best.

DAY 354

"I am enough, exactly as I am."

Action Step: Reflect on why you are worthy of love and acceptance, regardless of external achievements.

DAY 355

"I give myself permission to take up space."

Action Step: Stand tall, breathe deeply, and affirm your presence is valuable wherever you are today.

DAY 356

"I love myself unconditionally through every season of life."

Action Step: Write down one way you've supported yourself during a challenging time and express gratitude for your resilience.

_____

_____

_____

_____

_____

_____

DAY 357

"I celebrate my uniqueness and embrace who I am."

Action Step: Identify one quality that makes you unique and celebrate it by sharing it with someone.

DAY 358

"I am proud of how far I've come."

Action Step: Reflect on one major or minor accomplishment from the past year and honor your progress.

DAY 359

"I am kind to myself as I navigate life's ups and downs."

Action Step: Write down a mantra you can use when you feel overwhelmed or discouraged.

_____

_____

_____

_____

_____

_____

DAY 360

"I am my own greatest supporter and friend."

Action Step: Spend time today doing something you'd do for a close friend to show them love, but for yourself.

DAY 361

"I release harsh self-judgment and embrace self-compassion."

Action Step: Write down a negative thought you've had about yourself and reframe it with a compassionate perspective.

_____

_____

_____

_____

_____

_____

DAY 362

"I trust that I am doing my best with what I have."

Action Step: Reflect on one area where you've felt pressure or stress and remind yourself of your efforts.

DAY 363

"I take time to celebrate myself and my progress."

Action Step: Treat yourself to something you love today as a celebration of who you are.

DAY 364

"I love and accept every part of myself."

Action Step: Spend five minutes in front of a mirror, looking at yourself with love and repeating today's affirmation.

DAY 365

"I am a masterpiece in progress, always growing, always enough."

Action Step: Reflect on your journey of self-love and write a final gratitude note to yourself for showing up each day.

_____

_____

_____

_____

_____

_____

FINAL CHAPTER: YOUR JOURNEY OF JOY AND TRANSFORMATION

Celebrating your growth and embracing the future with joy.

Take a deep breath and pause for a moment—look how far you've come. Over the course of this book, you've taken intentional steps to reclaim your joy, rediscover your worth, and transform your life. You've cultivated gratitude, embraced courage, and built resilience. You've connected with your creativity, set boundaries, and opened your heart to healing. And through it all, you've shown up for yourself—day by day, moment by moment.

This final chapter is about celebration: celebrating the work you've done, the growth you've experienced, and the joy you've created. It's also about looking forward, carrying the lessons and affirmations you've embraced into every corner of your life.

Transformation is a lifelong journey, and while this book may come to an end, your journey continues. The tools, affirmations, and actions you've practiced here are always available to you, ready to support you through whatever comes next.

So let's reflect on your progress, honor your transformation, and set intentions for the bright, beautiful path ahead.

REFLECTION PROMPTS

Take a few moments to journal or meditate on the following questions:

1. **Looking Back**
   - What does joy mean to you now compared to when you started this journey?
   - Which chapter or theme resonated with you the most? Why?
   - How have your thoughts, actions, or habits shifted as a result of this journey?
2. **Celebrating Progress**
   - What is one thing you are most proud of about yourself?

○ How have you grown in your ability to face challenges, set boundaries, or express yourself?

○ Which affirmation or action step made the biggest difference for you?

3. **Looking Forward**

○ How will you continue to create joy and transformation in your life moving forward?

○ What areas of your life do you want to focus on next?

○ How will you hold yourself accountable for practicing what you've learned?

A VISION FOR THE FUTURE

Close your eyes and imagine the most joyful, fulfilling version of your life. Picture the relationships, experiences, and emotions that fill your days. What does your dream life look like? How does it feel to live it?

Write a letter to your future self, describing the life you are creating and the person you are becoming. Include affirmations, encouragement, and a promise to continue showing up for yourself every day.

CARRYING JOY FORWARD

Here's a reminder for the days ahead: You are your greatest resource. Every affirmation you've spoken, every action you've taken, has built a foundation of self-love, resilience, and empowerment. This foundation is yours to carry forward, a toolkit you can rely on no matter what life brings.

Keep practicing. Keep choosing joy. Keep believing in your ability to grow and transform. And most importantly, remember that this journey is not about perfection—it's about progress.

Whenever you need a reminder of your strength or a boost of inspiration, return to these affirmations. Let them anchor you, uplift you, and guide you as you navigate the beautiful, unpredictable path of life.

FINAL AFFIRMATION

"I am joy. I am transformation. I am enough."

Repeat this affirmation whenever you need to remind yourself of the incredible person you are and the remarkable journey you're on.

CLOSING ENCOURAGEMENT

Dear reader, you have done the work, and it shows. You've reclaimed your joy, transformed your mindset, and taken powerful steps toward living the life you deserve.

The best part? This is only the beginning. Your journey continues, and I can't wait to see all the beauty, strength, and joy you'll bring to the world.

With love, light, and endless joy,

Alesha Brown, The Joy Guru

Alesha Brown, The Joy Guru

ABOUT THE AUTHOR: ALESHA BROWN, THE JOY GURU

Alesha Brown, widely known as **Alesha Brown The Joy Guru**, is a shining example of resilience, transformation, and empowerment. As a survivor of childhood abuse, Alesha turned her pain into purpose, dedicating her life to helping others reclaim their joy, embrace their inner strength, and create lives of fulfillment and success. Her personal journey is a testament to the belief that no matter how difficult your past, joy, and transformation are always possible.

As a highly sought-after publisher, media mogul, and non-profit executive, Alesha is the CEO and founder of **Fruition Publishing Concierge Services**® and **Alesha Brown Productions**. Her publishing company empowers authors to monetize their expertise, craft impactful stories, and build legacies that inspire others. With Alesha Brown Productions, she expands her reach into film production, reality television, and speaking engagements, sharing stories that transform lives and create lasting impact.

In addition to her work as a publishing and media leader, Alesha serves as the COO of **Crusading Outreach Ministry, Inc.,** a nonprofit organization dedicated to uplifting underserved communities. Her work includes grant writing, offering resources, advocacy, and education on issues such as literacy, mental health awareness, and strengthening families. Through her leadership, Alesha provides a voice and support system for those who need it most, furthering her mission to empower others to overcome adversity and thrive.

Alesha's philosophy is simple yet profound: *"It is never too late to edit your life."* Whether she is coaching authors, mentoring nonprofit leaders, or creating empowering media content, Alesha is a living embodiment of this message.

Her latest book, **"Reclaim Your Joy: 365 Affirmations for Liberation and Transformation,"** is a daily guide to embracing happiness, building resilience, and creating a life of purpose. Through her affirmations and actionable steps, Alesha equips readers to navigate their challenges, rediscover their worth, and live boldly.

Alesha Brown's work inspires countless individuals to reclaim their power, dream fearlessly, and live authentically. Her life's mission is a reminder that no matter your past, your future is limitless.

TheJoyGuru.net

facebook.com/AleshaBrownTheJoyGuru

instagram.com/thejoyguru

tiktok.com/@thejoyguru

youtube.com/@AleshaBrownTheJoyGuru

threads.net/@thejoyguru